Pope John Paul II

Bringing Love to a Troubled World

by Anthony DiFranco

DILLON PRESS, INC.   MINNEAPOLIS, MINNESOTA

Library of Congress Cataloging in Publication Data

DiFranco, Anthony Mario.
 Pope John Paul II: bringing love to a troubled world.

 (Taking part)
 SUMMARY: A biography of the former Polish cardinal who was the first non-Italian to be elected Pope since 1523.
 1. John Paul II, Pope, 1920-   —Juvenile literature.
 2. Popes—Biography   —Juvenile literature.
 [1. John Paul II, Pope, 1920-   . 2. Popes] I. Title.
 BX1378.5.D53 1983 282'.092'4 [B] [92] 82-23618

 ISBN 0-87518-241-0

Dillon Press, Inc., 500 South Third Street
Minneapolis, Minnesota 55415
Printed in the United States of America
  2 3 4 5 6 7 8 9 10 91 90 89 88 87 86 85 84

The photographs are reproduced through the courtesy of Father M. Malinski (from Pope John Paul II: The Life of Karol Wojtyla, *published by Burns and Oates, Ltd., London, and Seabury Press/Crossroad, New York); Milton and Joan Mann—Cameraman International; Picture Group, Inc., Shepard Sherbell, photographer; and the Religious News Service. Photos on pages 50, 51, 52, 53, 54, 55 and 56 © L'Osservatore Romano, Servizio Fotografico, Citta' del Vaticano.*

Contents

POPE JOHN PAUL II

When Karol Cardinal Wojtyla was chosen as Pope John Paul II in 1978, he became the first non-Italian pope in 455 years. The brilliant Polish Catholic leader is a man of many talents and vocations—poet, actor, outdoorsman, patriot, and priest. He stands today as one of the great leaders of our times.

Growing up in the small farm town of Wadowice, Karol Wojtyla was known as a strong, handsome, and popular young man. As a promising young actor studying at a university in Kraków, he saw the Nazis invade Poland and murder 6 million Poles. The horror of the war and two close brushes with death led Karol to study for the priesthood. After the war, in a Poland ruled by Communists, he fought for the rights of Polish Catholics to practice their religion.

Wojtyla became the youngest Polish bishop and the second-youngest cardinal in the history of the Roman Catholic church. He played a key role in some of the new directions for the church made at the Second Vatican Council. As Pope John Paul II, he has traveled to many countries in an effort to renew the forces of love, justice, and peace in our troubled world. Wherever he has gone, he has brought a sense of goodness and hope and joy to the millions of people who have come to hear his message.

Karol Wojtyla greets the crowd in Saint Peter's Square after his election as Pope John Paul II.

1. A Small Town Polish Childhood

For two days the huge crowd had been waiting. Now at last it was time to hear the good news. TV lights blazed in the big square outside Saint Peter's Church in Rome as a hundred thousand people pressed forward. From the balcony, a priest began to speak in Latin. "We have a pope..."

The crowd gave a rousing cheer. Then there was a hush. All ears strained to hear the name of the Roman Catholic church's new leader: "Karol Cardinal Wojtyla *(Voy-tee-wah)*, who has taken the name John Paul II."

In that moment, the world was stunned. For hundreds of years, every pope had been an Italian. Now a Pole, a man from a Communist country, had been elected the leader of the world's largest church.

Carolus Joseph (Karol) Wojtyla was born on May 18, 1920, in Wadowice *(Va-do-vit-zeh)*, Poland, a small farm town 30 miles from the busy city of Kraków *(Crack-oov)*. Wheat, potatoes, and beets were brought to Wadowice from nearby farms for sale.

Karol's parents were not well off. His father was a supply officer in the Polish army, and his mother had been a teacher. Little "Lolek," as Karol was called, had one brother, Edmund, who was fifteen years older.

The Wojtylas lived in a plain stone building on a street corner in Wadowice. Three of their windows faced Saint Mary's Church across the street. For Karol this closeness to the church added to the already large place of religion in Polish life.

Karol's childhood home in the small town of Wadowice, Poland.

Like most country towns, Wadowice was a quiet place. But each Sunday its people came flocking to their six-hundred-year-old church for the Mass, or the "Lord's Supper." In the Mass, they believed, Jesus' sacrifice on the cross for all people was made real once more. Dressed in their best, they filled Saint Mary's to the doors.

From the beginning, Karol showed an interest in the church. Sometimes he played at saying Mass with his friends. His family prayed together every day, and on Sundays his father often walked him to church in his army uniform.

Later, Karol became an altar boy, which meant that he had the honor of helping the priest during Mass. The service was at seven in the morning. Afterward he had to run to get to school on time.

The school day lasted from eight in the morning until four in the afternoon. After school, Karol did homework or helped his mother. He was a very bright student. In fact, one teacher, Dr. Zacher, said, "He was the nearest to a genius that I ever taught." Another was even stronger in his praise: "He was the masterpiece of how a young man should be and act."

Karol liked to read and to help his friends with their studies. He was well liked and was such a good organizer that he even looked after the list of altar boys.

Karol, however, was far from being a book-worm. Sports and the outdoors were very impor-

Karol at the time of his first communion in the Roman Catholic church.

tant to him. In soccer he usually played goalie, and afterward he cooled off by swimming with his friends in the Skawa *(Ska-va)* River. One of the boys' favorite games was "palant," in which a player hits a stick in the air with another stick. Karol liked winter sports best of all, especially skiing on the hills around Wadowice.

Karol's childhood had some sad times, too. When he was nine, his mother died giving birth to a stillborn child.

Only four years later, the family suffered yet another blow. Edmund, Karol's brother, had become a doctor. He caught scarlet fever from one of his patients, and died.

Now Karol was alone with his father. Mr. Wojtyla, who had retired on a small army pension, was quite strict. "Fathers used their belts in those days," recalls Boguslaw *(Bo-gus-wav)* Banas, Karol's boyhood friend.

But Karol's father was also a good and warm-

Ten-year-old Karol Wojtyla (second from right in the back row) *with his father* (center, back row).

hearted man. He saw to it that Karol went to Mass every day and studied. He cooked, cleaned, and laundered for his son. After dinner, the two walked side by side in the town, always talking.

Karol was very friendly with his next-door neighbor, Mr. Kotlarczyk *(Kot-lar-chik)*, a teacher who designed sets for the theater. He started Karol's longtime interest in acting.

When Karol began high school, he joined the drama club. He acted in and directed plays, began to write poetry, and learned to play the guitar and sing.

Karol was a strong, handsome, and popular teenager. Even so, he didn't have much to do with girls. And though he loved the church, he didn't seem interested in the priesthood.

One day the archbishop of Kraków, Cardinal Sapieha *(Sap-yeh-ha)*, visited Wadowice. Karol, the high school's best student, gave a welcoming speech. Afterward Cardinal Sapieha spoke to him. "You seem to be a bright young man," said the cardinal. "Are you going to be a priest?"

"No," Karol said. "I am going to the university to study literature. And I'm interested in the theater, too."

"That's a pity!" exclaimed the cardinal. Happily for Cardinal Sapieha, Karol's answer was not his last word on the subject.

2. *The Test of War*

After high school, Karol moved to Kraków to continue his studies. In this lovely city, called "the jewel of Poland," Karol and his father lived in a dim basement apartment. For the summer, Karol worked with a road building crew. In the fall, he enrolled at the university.

The old Jageillonian *(Ya-gell-on-yan)* University, known as the UJ, was a splendid place. Rich in history, it was a perfect setting to study Polish art and writing. But history was about to catch up to the UJ, and all Poland. For Karol the timing was very bad.

Throughout their history, the Poles had not been a lucky people. In the past, the countries surrounding Poland had fought many wars on Polish lands. Since 1795, parts of Poland had been ruled by Austria, Prussia, and Russia. However, just before Karol's birth, its enemies were beaten in World War I, and Poland was made whole again.

Its wholeness, though, was far from steady. The new nation was poor, for many of its factories and workers had been carried off to other lands. In 1920 the Russian army invaded. Luckily, it was beaten back at Warsaw, Poland's capital. For a while, the Poles were free.

Their freedom, however, would not last for long. From the east, Communist Russia watched with greedy eyes. To the west, the Germans grew strong and land-hungry. Their new leader, Adolf Hitler, headed a warlike party called the Nazis. Poland itself was divided and weak. Only two things helped hold the country together. One was its rich heritage, or shared ways from the past, and the other was the Catholic church.

Both played a big part in Karol's life at the UJ. He joined theater groups, went to plays, and wrote poetry. And he also visited churches and held prayer meetings.

One dream came true when he won a part in a play, *The Knight of the Moon*. It told of a man who sold his soul to the devil and went to hell. After praying, he was let go and landed on the moon. Karol played the part of Taurus, the zodiac

Karol (third row, far left) *with other university students in Kraków.*

M. Malinski

bull. His costume was gym shorts, boxing gloves, and a bull's head.

Karol liked acting so much that he decided to make it his career. "Everyone was sure he would be an actor," a fellow student said. "He was very good."

But only a few weeks later, all of Karol's plans were turned upside down. What had been feared for years happened at last. Hitler's armies invaded Poland.

The struggle was short because Hitler's war machine was geared for "lightning attack." The Poles fought bravely, but their cavalry was no match for tanks. Within a month, they were beaten.

Hitler then made Poland a slave state to serve the needs of his armies. Its people were used for forced labor, and all universities, including the UJ, were closed. After all, slaves could not be allowed to think or have ideas. The Gestapo, or

Nazi secret police, rounded up teachers, priests, and leaders. Most were never seen again.

One day the Nazis called together the teachers from the UJ. They claimed that they wished to reopen the school. Instead, they arrested all the teachers who showed up, and many later died in prison camps.

It's hard to imagine what life in Poland was like during these times. Near Kraków the Nazis built a huge death camp, called Auschwitz *(Owshvits)*. Day and night, innocent Poles were dragged off and sent there to die in gas chambers. Some, like the teachers at the UJ, were Karol's friends. Within six years, more than 6 million Poles, one-fourth of the nation's people, were killed. About 3 million of the victims were Polish Jews.

Some young Poles were determined to continue their schooling as a way to fight back for Poland. Karol Wojtyla was one of them. While the Nazis were destroying schools and books, daring teachers and students started a secret, or "underground," university. Small groups met in private homes to hear lessons. In all, 136 teachers secretly taught classes for more than 800 students.

One meeting place was the home of Juliusz Kydrynski *(Yool-yush Kid-rin-skee)*, Karol's close friend. Once the Gestapo came to the house just before a meeting and saw all the chairs. "My mother said we were preparing for a party," Kydrynski recalls. "This seemed to satisfy them, and they left." If they had come during the meeting, Karol and his friends would have paid with their lives.

Like all students, Karol took a job to avoid arrest. He and Kydrynski worked in a quarry as stonecutters. Quarry work was very hard for young people who had never done it before. That winter the air was bitterly cold, and a meal for a whole day was often rye bread and jam. Yet Karol became a friend and leader to the workers.

Later in life he wrote a beautiful poem, "The Quarry," which showed the dignity and pain of working life.

During the winter, Mr. Wojtyla had a heart attack. One day Karol came home at lunchtime to find his father dead. Karol was shocked and deeply saddened, for he had grown very close to his father in their years alone. After the funeral, Karol seemed changed. Secretly, he took up his religious studies again.

Karol also formed an underground theater group. The arts, he knew, were important to Poland's survival. When his old neighbor, Kotlarczyk, moved to Kraków, the two joined forces to form the Rhapsodic Theater. This group boldly put on Polish plays for small gatherings in back rooms and cellars. Karol took part in seven plays.

But this was also a time of change in his life. Twice he had serious accidents. First his skull was injured when he was knocked down by a streetcar. As he lay between life and death, he felt a strong call to the priesthood. Still, he could not bring himself to give up the theater.

A few months later, Karol was badly hurt again when he was run down by a German truck. From that time on, his shoulder was stooped.

Lying in the hospital, Karol felt the call to the priesthood once more. This time, though, it was stronger. He had seen much horror since the Nazis came, and he had learned much about the world and himself. All the while, he had stayed close to the church. Now his life was at a turning point. After much thought and prayer, Karol made up his mind. Much as he loved acting, it would not be his career. Instead, he would become a priest.

To do so was to risk his life. The Nazis had closed down the schools for priests, called seminaries, and they had sent away or killed the students. Even so, Karol joined the UJ's secret seminary. For two years he kept up his studies and worked full time at the quarry.

Then, in August 1944, came the famous "Warsaw revolt." Hitler's armies had been losing ground in their war against the world, and they seemed close to defeat. Now the Russians were about to invade German-held Poland. They urged the Poles to rise up in arms. Together, said the Russians, they would push the Nazis out.

Though the Poles had few weapons, they had a great deal of courage. The people of Warsaw rose up against the Nazis. Sixty-three days later, the uprising was finally crushed. While two hundred thousand brave Poles died, the Russians stood by without coming to their aid.

Afterward the Nazis went mad with revenge. On August 6 they swarmed through Kraków, searching houses and dragging people out to shoot them. All day long the gunfire rang out. The Poles remember this day as "Black Sunday."

Karol was alone in his rooms, praying. Though his door was unlocked, he was spared.

But for Cardinal Sapieha, Black Sunday was too close a call. To protect his few priests-in-training, he took the risk of hiding them in his own palace. Once inside, Karol and the 19 others couldn't leave, for they were being hunted by the Nazis. For six months they studied, ate, and slept in the palace living room.

Sapieha was a brave and clever man. Once the German governor had himself invited to tea. He was served on the finest plates in the palace. The meal, however, was black bread and jam—the same poor food as that eaten by the hungry Poles! Another time, the governor looked through some of the palace's rooms. He had no idea that the hunted students were right under his nose.

At last, in January 1945, the horror ended. Russian armies swept through Poland, chasing the Nazis before them. Soon the war was over.

3. Growing with the Church

The end of the war did not bring peace for the Poles. Many feared that the Russians would become their new masters. Yet others were Communists and wanted ties with Russia. Soon the Poles were fighting with one another, while the Russian army stayed in Poland.

Once Karol was almost arrested by the Russians. He was singing Polish songs with a group of students in the Kraków marketplace, a daring act in the midst of Russian soldiers. Luckily, the students slipped away just in time.

Karol also joined a group that helped students get food and money. Soon he was one of its leaders. "He was very wise," a fellow student remembers. "I can't say that we guessed he would become pope. But we knew that somehow he was bigger than anybody else. Not just in size, but in every way."

Cardinal Sapieha knew that Karol was someone special, too. On November 1, 1946, he gave Karol his priestly vows. He was eager to send the bright young priest to Rome for special study. But first Father Wojtyla returned to Wadowice where his hometown friends were proud to hear a mass said by "little Lolek."

Afterward Father Wojtyla studied in Rome for two years, and he also spent time in Belgium, Holland, and France. All the while, his mind was challenged by new ideas and languages. "Each day is packed," he wrote to a friend. "This gives me the feeling that I am serving God according to my talents and His will....My heart is always close to Poland....I pray for her, read about her..."

But by the time he came home with his doctor's

degree, his country had changed. The Polish Communists had won control, and their government now answered to the harsh Russian ruler, Stalin.

The Communists believed that religion was bad for people. Since to them even the idea of God was evil, the church was their enemy. Yet most of Poland was deeply Catholic, which made it hard for the government to simply crush the church. Instead, it had to smother it slowly.

Such were the times when Father Wojtyla started work as a priest. His first church was in the country village of Niegowic *(Nyeh-go-vits)*. There the people listened spellbound to his preaching and praised him for his kindness. If a farmer was ill, Wojtyla took his place in the fields. "He was always wanting to do things for you," one old man said. "But we knew they'd soon take him from us. Clearly, he was going to be an important man."

Father Wojtyla with children from a church class in his first parish in Niegowic, Poland.

A year later, Wojtyla was moved to Saint Florian's church in Kraków. Here the people quickly grew to love him, too. They were surprised, though, by the strange ways their new priest had. He wore no overcoat, and his priest's robe was old and patched. Every gift, even a new coat, was turned over to the poor.

Wojtyla's life at Saint Florian's was very busy.

Students followed him everywhere, even to the movies, and children drew him into their street soccer games. On Sundays, crowds came to hear him preach in his deep voice. After the service they often saw him running to speak somewhere else. So many people wanted to hear him that his bed seemed hardly ever used.

After three years of this nonstop life, Wojtyla was moved again, to nearby Saint Catherine's church. Here his life was quieter. He studied for a second doctor's degree, and he wrote.

Karol Wojtyla had become a powerful thinker and a writer of books, essays, and poems. Love, work, marriage—these are the things he wrote about. For his poems alone, he might have been well known. Not all are religious, but they all show the dignity of God's creation. And they all search for the true meaning of life.

Here is the beginning of "The Quarry," the poem Karol wrote about working as a stonecutter.

M. Malinski

One of Karol's favorite places to read and think was outdoors among the hills and lakes of his native Poland.

Listen: the even knocking of hammers,

so much their own,

I project on to the people

to test the strength of each blow.

Listen now: electric current

cuts through a river of rock.

And a thought grows in me day after day:

the greatness of work is inside man.*

*From *Easter Vigil and Other Poems,* by Karol Wojtyla, translated by Jerzy Peterkiewicz

Since Father Wojtyla had been an actor, it's not surprising that he was a fine speaker, too. A dean from the University of Lublin *(Loob-lin)* was so impressed by his preaching that he hired him to teach classes there. Before long, the new teacher's classroom was jammed with students. His clear, simple words seemed to come to the heart of any problem. Wojtyla taught at Lublin for many years, refusing any payment.

But life was not all work. Father Wojtyla took his students on bicycle, ski, and kayak trips. Often they hiked in the hills, camping out at night. "Uncle," as the students called him, was the first to wake in the mornings. After taking a kayak ride alone, he would say mass on a turned-over boat.

These were peaceful times for Father Wojtyla. Perhaps the only sadness was the death of his old friend, Cardinal Sapieha. The peaceful times, however, would not last for long. One day mes-

(Above) *On a kayak trip with his students, Karol takes a peaceful, early morning ride.* (Right) *Karol enjoys the bright sun and fresh air of a kayak trip.*

sengers tracked him down on a kayak trip and brought him to Warsaw to see the cardinal primate, or Catholic leader, of Poland. "The pope has named you a bishop," he was told. "Will you accept?"

"Does this mean I can't finish my kayak trip?" Karol asked. The cardinal let him go back to the lakes. Right afterward, he was made a bishop of

Kraków. At 38 years of age, he was Poland's youngest bishop ever.

A bishop's job is very important. Karol Wojtyla, though, didn't want to change his simple ways, and he wanted to stay in his small apartment. Church leaders didn't agree. Waiting until he was out of the city, they moved his things into the bishop's palace. When the new bishop came home, he wasn't pleased. He moved again, into a small, plain room in the palace.

Bishop Wojtyla was an early riser who often worked a 16-hour day. Always he was reading, writing, and meeting people. He even had the back seat of his car turned into a little office.

The Roman Catholic church had need of such energy and skills. After only five years, Wojtyla was made an archbishop. Four years later, he became a cardinal, joining the church's highest leaders. At 47, Wojtyla was the second-youngest cardinal in church history.

As always, he was hard-working and kind. Cardinal Wojtyla said mass each morning at seven, and then prayed and wrote until eleven. After that, anyone could see him without an appointment. "One couldn't imagine a better person to work for," said Sister Jadwiga *(Yad-vee-ga)*, his assistant. "He never fussed or got angry."

As a cardinal, Wojtyla worked with Roman Catholic leaders from many countries. At times he traveled far from his homeland to talk with them about new directions in the life of the church.

4. *Fighting for the People*

During these years, the Catholic church went through an exciting change. In the Vatican, the church's headquarters in Rome, a special meeting, or "council," was called. Its goal was to make the church more up-to-date and aware of the needs of its members. Not in many years had the church taken on such a big task. It gathered its leaders from all over the world in the Vatican. The council, known as the Second Vatican Council, or Vatican II, lasted three years. Its paperwork took another seven to complete.

Vatican II changed the face of the church. Before it, priests had said the Mass in Latin, a very old language that was no longer spoken by many people. And during the Mass they stood before an altar facing away from the people.

After Vatican II, altars were turned around to face the people, and in many churches the native language was used instead of Latin. Even more important, the church began a reaching out to meet the real needs of its members. It made plans to help families, the old, and the sick. People were put before rules and ceremony.

Karol Wojtyla's clear, forceful thinking played a large part in the Second Vatican Council. For instance, he pointed out that the church should not simply preach. It should help people find the truth already in them. Ideas like these became the council's building blocks.

Later, Wojtyla took part in bishops' meetings called synods. Everywhere he traveled—Australia, Germany, America—church leaders were struck by him. Pope Paul VI made him a close friend, and in 1976 he was asked to give special

Cardinal Wojtyla played an important part in the decisions made by church leaders at the Second Vatican Council.

sermons for the pope and his staff.

Back home in Poland, Wojtyla put the ideas of Vatican II to work. He set up clinics for the sick and disabled and started a Family Institute.

Doing religious work in Poland was difficult, for the Communists were keeping up their war on the church. They changed the school day to leave no time for religious training. They kept Catholic children out of college, and kept Catholic workers from getting better jobs. Though the number of people was growing, they stopped the building of churches.

Cardinal Wojtyla fought back. "Poland's fate should not be decided by the non-believers against the will of the believers," he declared. "For we are all of us Poland. And we all wish to build our country, because we all love it."

To show the church's strength, Wojtyla helped plan a big celebration to mark Poland's one thousand years of Christianity. The government paid no attention to it. Instead, it promised to build one thousand schools.

Polish Catholics became really angry when they learned the government's plans for Nowa Huta *(No-va Hoo-ta)*, a new town near Kraków. Built around a huge steelworks, it had houses for two hundred thousand people. The government meant it to be a model Communist city. Since the Communists did not believe in religion, it would have no church.

The people of Nowa Huta didn't agree with the plans. They held Mass in the open, and loudly demanded a church. At last the government gave in and named a building site. But then it tried to change its mind, saying the site would be used for a school. The people took to the streets in protest. Soldiers were sent in with tear gas and machine guns to put down the uprising.

For seven years, with the help of Cardinal Woj- tyla, the people fought for their church. At last they won a new building permit. Since the government would supply no money, the people spent ten more years building the church with their own hands. Proudly, they topped it with a cross as high as they could make it.

Cardinal Wojtyla blessed the finished church. "This city of Nowa Huta was built as a city without God," he said. "But the will of God and of the workers has won out. Let us all take the lesson to heart."

One clear lesson was that Wojtyla was a match for the Communists. Today, a dozen masses are said every Sunday at Nowa Huta's church.

While Wojtyla was fighting to keep the church alive in Poland, another life and death struggle came to an end in Rome. Pope Paul VI died in August of 1978. Sadly, cardinals from around the world gathered at the Vatican to choose a new pope.

Though a papal election is a big event for the

whole world, it is done in great secrecy. To keep the voting free from pressure, the cardinals are shut away inside a Vatican palace. They promise to keep what happens there secret forever. Their special meeting, called a "conclave," may last for days. Once it starts, no one may leave or speak to those outside.

Meanwhile, huge crowds and TV crews wait in nearby Saint Peter's Square because they want to be there when the new pope is named. After all, few jobs in the world are as important as his. He leads the world's largest church, with 750 million members. To Catholics, his power has been handed down right from the first "pope," Saint Peter, who was Jesus' companion. On certain matters, therefore, his word is law. His views also carry weight with the rulers of many nations.

The August 1978 conclave did its work in a single day. Cardinal Albino Luciani was elected pope. He was a surprise choice—except for the

Roman Catholic cardinals enter Borgia Hall at the Vatican at the beginning of the conclave that elected Pope John Paul II.

fact that he was an Italian. For the past 455 years, all the popes had been Italian cardinals. It is said, though, that some non-Italians did get votes in the conclave. One was Cardinal Wojtyla.

The new pope chose the name John Paul. He was gentle, holy, and much loved—yet he would not be the church's leader for long. Popes are elected for life. But after just 33 days, John Paul died of a heart attack.

1978 was to be the "year of three popes." Once more a conclave was called, but this time the voting would not go as smoothly. The support for the two favorite Italian cardinals was so evenly split that neither one could win. Unless something changed, the cardinals would have to agree on some new, lesser-known man.

Experts wondered whether the "foreigner" from Poland would have a chance. This idea did not please Cardinal Wojtyla. "Why are you taking so many pictures of me?" he asked one reporter. He knew that becoming pope would mean leaving his homeland forever, and his thoughts were on the Polish people and their struggle. Yet he also knew that if the cardinals chose him as the next pope, he would have to accept.

The crowd of Italians in the square was ready for a long wait. They kept their eyes on the palace stovepipe. When smoke came from this pipe, they would know that the cardinals had been voting. Black smoke would mean that no name had won enough votes. White smoke, however, would mean that the church had a new pope.

Three times in the next two days, black smoke poured out. Three times the crowd stirred—and was disappointed. At last, the fourth time, a great cheer broke out. The smoke was white! Within minutes the crowd was surprised to learn that a non-Italian had been made pope. His name was Karol Wojtyla, and he came from the faraway Communist country of Poland.

5. Reaching Out to the World

An hour later, the new pope came outside in his white and gold robes. A strongly built man, he had a slight stoop and a heavy walk. His clear blue eyes looked out from a kindly face. For his new name as pope, he had chosen John Paul II.

Soon he spoke to the crowd in the square. "Dear brothers and sisters," he said to them in Italian. "...I was afraid to take this heavy duty. Yet I did so in the spirit of obeying our Lord...." Pope John Paul II's voice was strong, and his words rang out clearly and honestly to Catholics all over the world. By the end of his short speech, he had won the people's hearts.

Letters of goodwill flooded in from the leaders

The Polish pope waves at the crowd from a balcony overlooking Saint Peter's Square.

of many nations. In Poland people danced in the streets. How proud they were of their Wojtyla!

But John Paul's remark about a "heavy duty" was true. It is said that he wept when the cardinals elected him, for no longer would he live in Poland. His new home would be the Vatican, a tiny independent country inside the city of Rome. Its huddle of churches and palaces would be a far cry from the hills and lakes of Poland.

As always, John Paul made the best of the change. A youthful 58, he plunged at once into his work. Though newcomers can easily get lost in the maze of Vatican offices, John Paul showed right away who was running things. He popped without warning into offices and questioned people when their bosses weren't around. All key decisions, he handled in person. Like a sea captain, John Paul wanted a "tight ship."

Meanwhile, his warm, outgoing manner was the delight of the crowds. From the day he was

In the Vatican and around the world, Pope John Paul II has reached out to people of different races, nationalities, and ways of life. Wherever he has gone—Mexico, Poland, England, Ireland, Asia, Africa, and the United States—he has brought a sense of goodness and hope and joy to the millions who have come to hear his message. No pope in history has traveled more.

The pictures in this special collection of photographs show John Paul II with some of the people he has met, both at home in the Vatican and during his worldwide travels. Speaking to them in seven languages, singing songs with them, he has blessed and touched as many as possible. In sun and snow, in east and west, in war and peace, he has brought love to a troubled world.

crowned pope, he showed his love of the people. Refusing the special pope's chair, he walked into the crowd and shook hands, kissed babies, and touched sick people. This was the new pope's way—a reaching out.

Soon the Vatican was mobbed by visitors as never before. Every Wednesday, as many as fifty thousand people gathered to see John Paul.

This huge crowd came to the Vatican to hear Pope John Paul II deliver his Easter message to the people of Rome and the world.

Speaking to them in seven languages, singing songs with them, he blessed and touched as many as possible. So many people came that the time of these gatherings had to be changed to avoid traffic jams.

As pope, John Paul was also the bishop of Rome. Unlike past popes, he did not see this as a minor duty. Each Sunday he visited a different church, and he also went to hospitals, schools, and poor sections of the city. Once a street sweeper's daughter asked him to perform her wedding. He agreed. Another time he tried to shake hands with a Vatican gardener. "They're dirty, Holy Father," the stunned man said, hiding his hands. "Yes, but I don't do my own washing," John Paul answered. He grabbed the man's hands and wiped them on his white robe.

John Paul reached out beyond Rome to the people of the world. He began his many travels as pope nearly right away with a visit to Mexico. On

During his first journey as pope, Karol Wojtyla makes friends with an Indian child in a village near the city of Oaxaca, Mexico.

arriving, he knelt and kissed the soil. This way of "reaching out" became a custom in all his visits.

In Mexico John Paul drove through cities and small villages. From windows, rooftops, and trees the crowds shouted "*Viva el Papa!*" ("Long live the pope!") John Paul said masses, visited hospitals, and listened to people's problems. Above all, he spoke against the unfairness and greed that kept many of the world's people poor and hungry. By the time his airplane left, 19 million Mexicans had seen him.

In all his travels, John Paul went through a whirlwind of masses, speeches, and rallies. Before long he had traveled more than one hundred thousand miles to Africa, Asia, South America, Ireland, and Eastern Europe. No pope in history had traveled more. His goal was to renew the force of love in our troubled world.

A visit to Poland was high on John Paul's list. When he arrived, cheering crowds turned out to greet him. Half a million Poles heard him say mass at the shrine of the "Black Madonna," the holiest in Poland. In Kraków a million people sang the Polish song "Sto-lat" for him. Its words wish a person 100 years of life.

For John Paul, the trip to Poland would not have been complete without a stop at his hometown of Wadowice. He prayed there for his dead parents, brother, and stillborn sister. After mass, one hundred thousand young people joined him in a lively songfest.

The Polish government was embarrassed by John Paul's visit. Though it would not let him stop at the church at Nowa Huta, it couldn't silence him. In his speeches, John Paul urged Poland's Communist leaders to respect the people's "basic human rights."

Later, these ideas about human rights helped to start a "Polish Spring." Some workers, demanding more freedom, formed their own trade union,

On his trip to Poland, John Paul II prays at the Wall of Death in the Auschwitz camp where Nazi prisoners were whipped, clubbed, and shot.

called "Solidarity." John Paul helped them by meeting with their leader, Lech Walesa, in Rome.

Solidarity's growing success showed how weak the Polish government was. For a while, it seemed that the old, harsh system might be changed. But then the army was called in to stop the workers, and Walesa and other leaders were jailed. Walesa has been freed, but Solidarity has been replaced by government-approved unions. And yet, after such an awakening, the Polish Spring does not seem likely to simply die.

In October 1979, John Paul spent seven days touring the United States. Tens of millions turned out in rain and mud to see him. When crowds chanted "We love you," he called back "I love you more."

John Paul visited Boston, New York City, Philadelphia, Des Moines, Chicago, and Washington, D.C. In one week he made 72 speeches! Often his thoughts were meant for the young people in the audience. "Do not be afraid of honest effort and honest work. Do not be afraid of the truth," said the pope. He warned against trying to escape in drugs and selfishness.

Young people could not mistake John Paul's love for them. "*Wooo—wooo!*" he would call into the microphone. This is a loving sound that Polish parents make at their children. Twenty thousand teenagers filled New York's Madison Square Garden to see him. They gave him gifts of jeans, T-shirts, and a guitar. John Paul called the jammed, happy arena "a garden of life."

At the United Nations in New York City, John Paul spoke against the arms race. In the Midwest, he praised America's farmers. But not everything he had to say was easy. John Paul stood strongly behind the church's strict rules against divorce, birth control, and abortion. He also said that the rules for the priesthood must not be changed. "Priesthood is forever," he re-

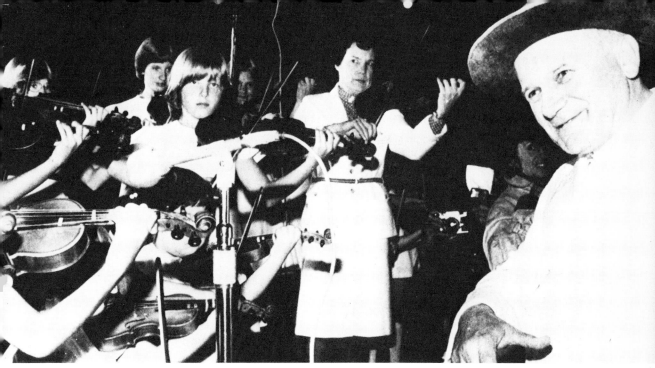

In Chicago the pope listens to the young violinists of the Suzuki Academy of the Performing Arts.

minded priests in Philadelphia. "We do not return the gift once given."

This firmness disappointed some Catholics. After Vatican II, they had hoped for more changes in some of the church's old rules. John Paul's views centered on the dignity of each person. But he also seemed determined to lead the church back onto its proven course.

One Catholic nun, Sister Theresa Kane, protested in public in Washington, D.C. During a welcoming speech for John Paul, she urged that women, too, be allowed to be priests. Taken by surprise, John Paul smiled faintly. In his own speech, he said plainly that the priesthood was for men. But women had "an important place in the church" as well, and he urged nuns to keep up their good work. Later, another group of nuns apologized for Sister Kane's "rudeness."

After a final mass in the Washington Mall, John Paul returned to Rome. His tiring world-wide travels continued, and so did his reaching out to huge crowds in the Vatican. Standing in his white jeep, called the "Popemobile," John Paul would ride among the people. He would shake hands and scoop up babies.

During such a happy moment, on May 13, 1981, a gunman, hiding in the crowd, shot at John Paul. Two bullets wounded the pope in the abdomen, arm, and hand. He fell back, bleeding. While he was rushed to the hospital, the gunman,

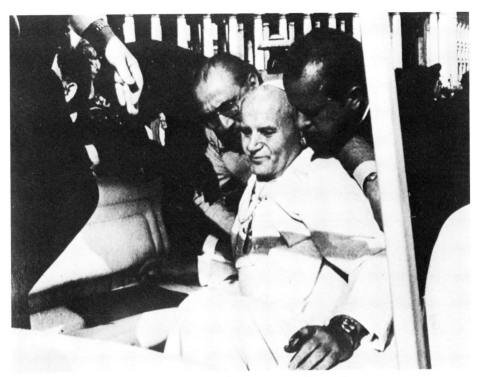

John Paul II just after he was shot by a young Moslem terrorist.

a young Moslem terrorist, was caught. A murderer, he had escaped from jail in Turkey and thought of the pope as his enemy. The world was horrified by his act.

At first John Paul's life was in danger. After a long operation, he spent months getting well. The gunman was sentenced to life in prison by a Rome court. John Paul, though weak, forgave him.

Later another operation was needed to mend John Paul's wounds. But within a year, he was as active as ever. Again he mixed with the crowds, though now not as freely as before. And again he worked long, hard days in the Vatican and on trips.

John Paul's busy day starts at five in the morning. After a time of private prayer, he says Mass at seven in a Vatican chapel. His breakfast, fixed by a cooking staff of six Polish nuns, is usually ham and eggs. Sometimes guests share it with him.

Next come church business and private meetings. At lunch John Paul's guests are often bishops from far-off countries. They may be surprised at his deep gaze and pointed questions. After a midday nap, John Paul works until dinner. While eating, he reads news reports and watches TV news shows, and then he works into the night.

His worldwide travel is added to this tiring

schedule. Four years after becoming pope, John Paul had already taken 15 trips. Some have made history.

For instance, his six-day visit to Great Britain in May 1982 was the first ever for a pope. It raised hopes of a rejoining of the Catholic church and Church of England. The two churches had split apart 450 years before. During his visit, John Paul met with the queen of England, and he shared a church service with the archbishop of

At Gatwick Airport near London, the pope greets well wishers at the start of his mission of peace to Great Britain.

Canterbury, the leader of the Church of England. The two men exchanged gifts and hugs. "My dear brothers and sisters...whom I love and long for," John Paul greeted the people. Two million of them in nine cities turned out to see him.

John Paul brought another message with him, for Britain and Argentina were at war. Again and again, John Paul spoke against the fighting. "War should belong to the tragic past, to history," he said.

Within weeks, John Paul traveled to Argentina, too. All wars are "always unjust," he told the people there. When he was leaving, a crowd of two million shouted "We want peace."

In the same month, John Paul received a visit from President Reagan of the United States. The president spoke of his concern for the struggles within Poland. John Paul called on America "to fulfill its mission in the service of world peace."

This tireless seeking for peace is perhaps John

Paul's greatest gift as pope. Though in his sixties, he still works tirelessly to bring the power of love to a troubled world. His travels take him from one hot spot to another. Often there is danger. Again, on a visit to Portugal, he was attacked by a man with a knife. This time he was unharmed. His message remains unchanged: "Violence is a lie, for it goes against the truth of our faith, the truth of humanity."

John Paul II stands today as one of the great leaders of our times. Poet, actor, outdoorsman, priest—his life has been made of many parts. But there is a oneness that unites them all. From the days when he prayed with his parents as a child, Karol Wojtyla has always been close to God. He has always found a way to see the goodness of the world. More than any other pope, John Paul II has brought this sense of goodness and hope to young people. He has reminded the world that joy is the heart of the Christian message.

The Author

Anthony Mario DiFranco's short stories and articles have appeared in a variety of publications, and his short story, "The Brave," won the Catholic Press Association's first prize for fiction in 1981. He is also the author of *Italy: Balanced on the Edge of Time*, published by Dillon Press. The author credits his large extended family for providing him with abundant writing material. In addition, he has had a long acquaintance with and interest in the Roman Catholic church.

  Born in New York City, Mr. DiFranco studied at Fordham University where he received a B.A. in classical languages and an M.A. in English, and at Saint John's University, where he earned a professional diploma in school administration. Since 1974, the author has taught writing, literature, and journalism in the English department of Suffolk County Community College. He lives in Northport, New York, with his wife Adrienne and their four children.